NOT-FOR-PARENTS

# AUSTRALIA
## Everything you ever wanted to know

Janine Scott

Peter Rees

# CONTENTS

I'M COMING RIGHT BACK!

I'M FEELING A BIT BLUE... AND PINK AND YELLOW.

# NOT-FOR-PARENTS

**THIS IS NOT A GUIDEBOOK.** And it is definitely Not-for-parents.

**IT IS THE REAL, INSIDE STORY** about one of the world's most exciting countries—Australia. In this book you'll hear fascinating tales about **toothy sharks**, giant rocks and snappy crocs, **bushranger baddies**, and explorers galore.

Check out cool stories about a famous coat hanger, **underground hotels**, a super-fast horse, and a very rough race. You'll find flying doctors and flying fruit flies, **flesh-eating spiders**, and thieving convicts.

This book shows you an **AUSTRALIA** your parents probably don't even know about.

# THE LAND OF BiG

Australia does things in a big way. There are big crocs with big teeth and big kangaroos with big pockets. There are big reefs, big rocks, and big roads. And if you take a big road trip, give a big wave to the Big Banana, the Big Koala, and even the Big Prawn. Australia has six states and two territories, and each is bold, beautiful, and BIG!

## Big crocs

The Northern Territory is home to the biggest crocodiles, and none is bigger than the 26ft (8m) tall Big Boxing Crocodile statue in Humpty Doo!

## Big hole

A big meteorite made a big crater in the Kimberley region in Western Australia. Wolfe Creek Crater—2,870ft (875m) across—was big news in 1947 when it was spotted in an aerial survey.

Western Australia

## Big red

The big red center has the big, red rock Uluru, but it also has a big sand dune called the Big Red. You can play golf on it. What a big sand bunker!

## Big throw

If you could throw a boomerang from west to east across Australia, it would go the big distance of nearly 2,485mi (4,000km).

INDIAN OCEAN

## Big strides
An emu is a big bird that can take a 9ft (2.7m) leap forward but not even a small step backward.

## Big post
The world's longest postal run in a day flies from Cairns to Cape York. It takes a big nine hours, and there are 10 big stops on the way.

CORAL SEA

Northern Territory

Queensland

## Big sea
Imagine a post office in the big, blue sea! The Great Barrier Reef, 1,250mi (2,010km) long and the world's biggest group of coral reefs, has the only floating post office in Australia.

New South Wales

## Big road trips
Catherine Gregson was the first woman to drive around the big continent in 1937. Her mother went on the six-month trip with her. What a big help!

South Australia

★Australian Capital Territory

Victoria

TASMAN SEA

## Big divide
The Dingo Fence is the biggest fence in the world. It stretches about 3,490mi (5,615km) from South Australia to Queensland.

## Big devils
The biggest population of Tasmanian devils lives in Tasmania. That's because that's the only place they live!

Tasmania

WANT MORE?

**Australian stories, facts, and figures** ★ www.australia.gov.au/about-australia

# FiRST ARRiVALS

The first people came to Australia from Southeast Asia about 60,000 years ago, at a time when sea levels were low and Australia was part of a larger continent, called Sahul. These tall, slender arrivals probably parked their rough boats on the beach and wondered what they had let themselves in for! Ahead of them lay a vast, hostile landscape, full of strange new creatures that seemed determined to sting and bite them. It may have taken generations, but they would eventually find a niche as superb hunter-gatherers and custodians of the secrets of this ancient place.

"Indigenous Australians" means Aboriginal and Torres Strait Islander peoples, who are two distinct groups.

I'LL BE BACK.

### Killer kylie
The new continent was full of weird and delicious animals. Lizards and snakes could be caught through cunning and patience. Kangaroos and emus were quicker, but the hunters had a secret weapon: the kylie. Not the pint-sized Australian pop princess—this kylie was a killer boomerang that could stop a kangaroo dead in its tracks.

GO, KYLIE!

*Cathy Freeman*

## Flying the flag

The Aboriginal flag symbolizes the Indigenous people and their relationship to the land. Today, it is an official flag of Australia. But back in 1994 it caused a few flutters when gold-medalist Cathy Freeman proudly posed with it at the Commonwealth Games.

## Digging up the past

Australia's oldest man was discovered at Lake Mungo in New South Wales in 1974. Mungo Man lived about 42,000 years ago. From his bones, scientists believe he stood nearly 6.5ft (2m) tall, which makes Mungo humungous!

## Drone-pipe

Indigenous Australia has a unique voice—the growl of the didgeridoo. These ancient instruments are cut from hollowed out trees, although you can make a decent "didge" from PVC pipe! Listen carefully to the didgeridoo's drone and you will hear the sounds of the Aboriginal world—from a kangaroo's hop to a kookaburra's cackle.

## BIG TIME

- ✫ About 60,000 years ago: first humans in Australia
- ✫ 42,000 years ago: Mungo Man lived and died
- ✫ 20,000 years ago: earliest known rock art, at Koonalda Cave
- ✫ 5,000 years ago: the dingo introduced from Asia as a pet
- ✫ 1606: first contact with Europeans
- ✫ Late 18th century: Indigenous population is approximately 500,000, with about 500 groups speaking 300 languages
- ✫ Early 20th century: population plunges below 100,000
- ✫ 2006: Indigenous population has grown to 517,000

BY JINGO, I'M A DINGO!

WANT MORE?

**Mungo National Park, home of Mungo Man** ✫ www.visitmungo.com.au

# LIFESAVERS FOR LIFE

If you see a lifesaver racing into the surf to pluck a swimmer to safety, you can thank William Gocher, who had only mutiny on his mind when he went for a swim one Sunday at noon at Manly Beach in Sydney. The year was 1902, and the law stated that swimming was strictly forbidden every day during daylight hours. The defiant Mr. Gocher, who had been defiant for three Sundays in a row, was arrested. However, it was the beginning of the end of the ludicrous law. But where there are swimmers, there are people who need to be rescued. Five years after William Gocher's daring dips, the first surf lifesaving clubs in the world splashed onto the scene.

IF WE CAN'T SEE YOU, WE CAN'T SAVE YOU.

I CAN SEE SOMEONE WAVING, OR IS IT JUST A WAVE?

**Roped in to rescue**
Today, motorized rescue boats roar to the rescue up and over the wild white waves. Early rescue devices consisted of a life jacket tied to a piece of rope. What a lifesaver!

### Little lifesavers

Nippers is a junior surf lifesaving program that teaches surf skills to children aged between five and thirteen. In 1977 girls could join the Nipperettes. Women, however, could not become active patrolling members of a surf club until 1980. You're kidding!

### Flags in a flap

You wouldn't want to be a color-blind swimmer. In some countries, the flag that goes up when a shark has been spotted is blue and purple. That might make you see red!

### Between the flags

Swimmers are advised to swim between the yellow-and-red flags. This is the safer part of the beach and is patrolled by lifesavers. Mind you, there's nothing stopping sharks from swimming between the flags, too. So if a red-and-white checkered flag goes up and a siren goes off, be alarmed! It means a shark is also patrolling the beach.

The world's first surf lifesaving club started at Sydney's Bondi Beach in 1907.

### A REEL STORY

Who would have thought that a simple cotton reel would help save swimmers' lives. In 1906 Lyster Ormsby, a member of the lifesaving club at Bondi Beach, was a "reel" lifesaver! He built a model of the now famous lifesaving reel out of a cotton reel and two hairpins. A year later, full-sized reels were used to pull swimmers to safety.

MY ARMS ARE REEL-Y, REEL-Y TIRED.

WANT MORE?

**Surf Life Saving Australia official site** ☆ www.sls.com.au

# THE COAT-HANGER CROSSING

John Job Crew Bradfield was a small man who liked to think BIG. Known as the "father" of the Sydney Harbour Bridge, Bradfield's vision stretched far into the future when he planned a bridge with six road traffic lanes, four railroad lines, and two wide footways. At the time of the bridge's completion in 1932, many people still rode horses and buggies! But not even Bradfield could have predicted that a staggering 250,000 vehicles would cross the "coat-hanger" every single day.

*IT DOESN'T LOOK LIKE A COAT HANGER TO ME.*

John Job Crew Bradfield

*SORRY TO CUT IN!*

Captain Francis De Groot

## A riveting fact
There are six million rivets holding the bridge together. During construction, quality-control inspectors insisted that 101,559 rivets be removed and replaced. Wouldn't that drive you nuts!

## DANGEROUS WORK
In 1930 one lucky worker, Vincent Kelly, survived a 170ft (52m) fall from the arch, thanks to some skills he had picked up as a diver. He was declared for this fantastic feat "boilermaker of the year" and was presented with a gold watch and medal. Some say he received more than that though— the experience is said to have left him with a s-s-s-stutter!

## The ribbon robber
There was much pomp and ceremony at the bridge's opening on March 19, 1932. Captain Francis De Groot rode in on a horse, raised his sword, and slashed through the ribbon, declaring the bridge open. There was one slight problem. He wasn't an official, so he was carted off and charged under the Lunacy Act. The ribbon was retied and cut again!

*Diamond and coat-hanger lights celebrate its 75th birthday, 2007*

*WE'RE WHEEL-Y HEAVY!*

BridgeClimb Sydney

### Under, up, and over

Boats and ships go under the bridge every day. But in 1943, the Air Force flew some planes under it. One pilot changed his mind at the last minute and decided to fly over it. He nearly didn't make it. Today, people can walk up to the very top.

### Four feet across

Cars, trucks, buses, taxis, and trains zoom across the bridge. But in the early days, not everything that crossed over it had wheels. Sheep and pigs crossed for one penny a head. Horses and cattle cost two pence each. In April 1932, six elephants strolled across for two pence a piece.

WANT MORE?

**BridgeClimb Sydney official site** ★ **www.bridgeclimb.com**

Arctic Ocean

The *Surrey*

I'M SICK OF THE SEA!

### Sick at sea
In 1814 typhus swept through the *Surrey*, killing 36 convicts. The ship's captain could do nothing because he died of the disease too. A volunteer from another ship navigated the stricken *Surrey* to port.

# THE SAILING JAILS

In England back in the late 1700s, if you were a light-fingered thief but not very light-footed, chances are you would find yourself in the hands of the law. But with the jails full to the brim with crims, the next step was often a one-way ticket to Australia on a convict ship. There was nothing shipshape about these vessels. They were dark, dank and, of course, they stank. People couldn't wash, and many suffered from terrible seasickness.

The First Fleet, Sydney Cove, 26 January 1788

### Forget me not
The convicts would often spend months, even years, on a prison ship, called a hulk, before setting sail. To ensure their loved ones did not forget them, some convicts carved messages into copper pennies. These love tokens were called "leaden hearts."

DIDN'T A COPPER GET YOU HERE IN THE FIRST PLACE?

The First Fleet was delayed four times, so it left England seven months late.

## Keys in the sea

The prison doors below deck were kept locked. In 1822 a second mate aboard the *Eliza* who had just locked up was swept overboard to his death. Unfortunately, he had the only set of keys! The doors were opened by picking the locks.

# THE CONVICT CONVOY

The First Fleet convoy carried convicts from England to Australia. It set off on May 13, 1787 and consisted of six convict ships, three store ships, and two naval ships. During the journey, which took eight months and one week, there was high drama on the high seas.

1. ***Scarborough***—208 male convicts; the convicts tried to seize the ship two weeks into the journey
2. ***Friendship***—76 male convicts, 21 female convicts; it wasn't as friendly as its name suggests—fights were common, even between the officers and surgeons
3. ***Prince of Wales***—49 female convicts, 1 male convict; strong winds tore the sails and she even collided with the *Friendship*
4. ***Charlotte***—88 male convicts, 20 female convicts; a slow ship that had to be towed for the first week
5. ***Alexander***—195 male convicts; the convicts and the crew attempted a mutiny
6. ***Lady Penrhyn***—101 female convicts; there was nothing ladylike about some of the convicts, who had their hair cut off and their heads shaved for punishment.

## Dead leg

Convicts were often locked up in leg irons during the voyage. The more severe a convict's crime, the heavier the leg irons. That sure made convicts toe the line!

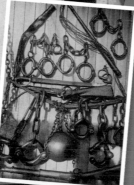

WANT MORE?

Convict facts and tales ★ www.convictcentral.com

# TEETH OF TERROR

There are fish-crunching, morsel-munching sharks bringing grief to the reefs all over Australia, and when their death-delivering dentures wear out or get lodged in a frightened fish, then there's another row of teeth ready to rip!

**Maim's my middle name**
Good grief, look at those teeth! A great white shark is also nicknamed the "white death." No wonder, really. It has about 240 razor-sharp teeth with jagged edges.

### What a blast!
Imagine dodging bombs and bullets while body surfing. In 1935 people were asked to suggest ways to help reduce shark attacks. Some of the more outlandish ideas were to use explosives to blow up the sharks or to mount machine guns up on the cliffs.

More people die surfing than from shark attacks.

### The cage of death
All this steel stops shark cage divers from becoming a shark meal. This is not for the fainthearted. There are no creature comforts in the cage and lunch is optional!

WANT SOME FISH FINGERS?

WHAT A TOURIST TRAP!

Jagged edge

## TEETH ON THE REEF

Different sharks have different kinds of teeth, depending on what they eat. Some teeth are designed to crush the shells of crabs and sea urchins. Some are smooth and rounded for grinding. Others just grab and stab!

## SHARK PARK

What would you expect to see at Shark Bay in Western Australia? Sharks, of course. One kind is called the nervous shark. What's it got to be nervous about? Maybe the peculiar-looking sharks that share its home.

> Between 1791 and 2012 there were 887 shark attacks in Australia; 215 were fatal.

> WHERE'S THE TOOTH FAIRY WHEN YOU NEED HER?

### Head like a hammer
Hammerhead sharks really nail their victims! They use their flattened heads to hold down their prey before they take a bite.

### Dead on the seabed
At Coogee Aquarium in 1935, a tiger shark vomited up an arm. Fingerprints and a tattoo on the arm led police to a small-time crook who had been dumped at sea.

> THAT TRUNK LOOKS 'ARMLESS.

### Tiger teeth
Tigers bite, and so do tiger sharks. In fact, sometimes people are on a tiger shark's menu!

WANT MORE?

Shark Bay ☆ www.sharkbay.org

# THE IRON OUTLAW

In the late 1800s, the thought of having bushrangers roaming around made some folks jumpy. So much so that one man, upon hearing a loud bang, hid up in a tree all night, only to discover in the morning that his cook had dropped a pot! The police were jumpy, too. After all, Ned Kelly, the infamous outlaw, had robbed banks and murdered three policemen. But at Glenrowan in 1880, the police took on the armed and armored Kelly Gang and won. Three of the gang lay dead, including Ned's brother Dan. Ned Kelly was wounded during capture. When Ned was hung later that year, he is reported to have said, "Such is life!"

## A LONG LETTER

In February 1879 the Kelly Gang headed to Jerilderie to rob a bank. The robbery took a few days. On Saturday night they locked up the two policemen in their own jail and waited for the bank to open on Monday. On Sunday Ned Kelly read his now famous 7,500-word letter to one of the policemen's wives. It explained how he wanted justice for himself and his family.

I AM NOT A LETTER BOX!

### Farmer armor
The Kelly Gang's armor was made from the curved blades of farm plows. Ned's suit was the heaviest and weighed 97lb (44kg). Where did they get hold of the plow blades? They bought some, pinched some, and farmers even gave them some.

### Treasure or trash?
The Kelly Gang's armor and helmets went to four different locations, except three of them got muddled up. Not everyone thought Ned Kelly's stuff was treasure. In the 1950s someone at a museum threw out his shotgun thinking it was junk!

Carrington

"E. KELLY?"
"NED" IS SHORT
FOR EDWARD.

**£8000 REWARD**
ROBBERY and MURDER.

## DEAD NED

Ned was hanged in Melbourne Gaol (Jail) on November 11, 1880. During Ned's autopsy, his head was cut off. In the 1920s rumor has it that his skull was a paperweight on a policeman's desk. In 1978 the skull was stolen from the Old Melbourne Gaol. Here is the latest heads-up. In 2009 the skull, which had "E. Kelly" written on the side, was handed in, but forensic scientists concluded that it wasn't Ned's head.

The reward for Ned Kelly's capture was split among 67 people!

THAT STANDS FOR "REALLY IMPORTANT PERSON."

R.I.P.

### Bones and bullets

At the autopsy, people took parts of the body for souvenirs. What was left of it was buried in a mass grave in the prison grounds. In 2011 scientists tested the bones of the 34 skeletons from the grave. They identified Ned Kelly's headless skeleton.

WANT MORE?

Ned Kelly ☆ www.ironoutlaw.com

# THE GiANT RED ROCK

Uluru rises about 1,130ft (345m) above the ground.

There is one rock in Australia that really rocks. Uluru is such a mammoth slab of red rock that you can hardly miss it, or can you? In 2006 one man, who was just 330ft (100m) away from it, waved down some passing police officers to ask for directions to it! The early European explorer Ernest Giles, who first saw the rock from a distance in 1872, described it as "the remarkable pebble." But one explorer who did see its mighty height up close was William Gosse. He named it "Ayers Rock," and in 1873 became the first European to rock up to the top.

CAN YOU SEE ULURU YET?

### To climb or not to climb?
The Indigenous owners of Uluru ask that people do not climb the rock because it is sacred, but they do not stop people from doing so. One of the recommendations, though, is that people who are scared of heights do not attempt the climb. Sensible advice. Uluru is the height of a 95-story building!

## LIGHTING UP THE ROCK

The giant rock may have eroded and changed over millions of years, but the light can make its color change throughout the day. It can alter from its famous red to appear orange or purple at sunset. It can also look silvery gray in the rain.

### Up and under

Ever heard of an iceberg in a desert? Uluru is like an iceberg because the rock that is visible above the ground is just part of the entire rock. About two-thirds of it lies underground.

WHERE THE DEVIL DID THOSE ANTS GO?

Thorny devil

### Ant trails

People look like tiny ants beside towering rocks. The local Indigenous people call the thousands of tourists who come to admire the rocks in the region "minga," or "ants!"

### A rocky road

These lizards are little devils, at least that is what all the ants at Uluru think. Thorny devils stalk ant trails and snap up the ants (the six-legged ants, that is) as they march past.

### Uluru who?

In 1993 its official name became Ayers Rock/Uluru. Then in 2002 it became Uluru/Ayers Rock. Good to get that settled.

THIS ROCK MAKES ME LOOK LIKE AN ANT!

WANT MORE?

# CROC SHOCK!

Menacing mosquitos might seem the peskiest problem on a camping trip, but what about a 11.5ft (3.5m) killer croc? A family camping in Kakadu National Park in 2006 got the shock of their life when a crocodile tried to trespass into their tent. The croc got a shock, too, and ended up crashing into a tree. That time, the croc came off second best. However, this is often not the case in crocodile country where crocs are the kings—and killers. Crocodiles have sunk their teeth into people, boats and even lawn mowers. Luckily for some people, their crocodile encounters have had happy—not snappy—endings!

HMMM, I THINK I LEFT MY RUBBER BAND AT HOME.

Crocodile statue, Australia Zoo

**Open wide**
Crocodiles have powerful muscles that snap their jaws shut with incredible force, but the muscles that open their jaws are weak. So remember to carry a thick rubber band in your pocket. Amazingly, that's all you need to secure your future.

# SALTIE VS. FRESHIE

There are two kinds of crocodiles in Australia:

**Saltwater crocodile:**
* ✫ biggest reptile in the world
* ✫ breeds in the wet season
* ✫ lives in fresh and salt water
* ✫ can grow up to 20ft (6m) long
* ✫ aggressive and will attack people

**Freshwater crocodile:**
* ✫ breeds in the dry season
* ✫ lives in fresh or slightly salty water
* ✫ can grow up to 10ft (3m) long
* ✫ shy, so stays away from people

*Saltwater crocodile*

## Smile, crocodile

Are crocodile teeth clean? Scientists in Australia are studying bacteria on crocodile teeth in order to produce better antibiotics for croc bites. A screwdriver holds the crocodile's mouth open while it has its dental work done—and stops it from saying, "See you later, alligator!"

> I'LL TRY TO GIVE THEM THE BRUSH OFF!

## Watch out

It sounds like something out of a Captain Hook movie, but swimming out there could be tick-tock croc. In 2004 a crocodile attacked an 11-year-old girl in Queensland. Thanks to a brave rescuer, who didn't let a second tick by, the girl survived the attack. Her watch was not so lucky. It was never heard from again!

## King of the crocs

In December 2011 Elvis the croc was feeling cranky when one of the keepers at the Australian Reptile Park north of Sydney mowed the grass in his enclosure. So Elvis mowed down the Victa lawn mower and dragged it into his lagoon. Elvis lost two teeth on the whirling blades and the lawn mower lost its job!

> I'M VINCE, NOT VICTOR!

## In the fast lane

Crocodiles are good swimmers, so you wouldn't think they would need to go to swimming boot-camp. In 2011 a small freshwater crocodile was found swimming among oblivious bathers in a public pool in Darwin. The croc was very considerate. It stayed in its own lane!

> I CAN RUN RINGS AROUND THEM.

WANT MORE?

Home of Elvis the crocodile ✫ www.reptilepark.com.au

# THE STATION NATION

Is it sensible to wear a woolen coat in temperatures that soar above 95°F (35°C)? Well, the millions of sheep in Australia might not think so, but they don't really bleat about it! It is not just sheep that have to beat the heat on the farms and stations. Cattle battle with it, too. Luckily, farmers have ways of dealing with what the weather throws at them. Mind you, that is not always easy in places where it gets so sizzling in summer that tires can explode.

WHEN WILL I BE SHAUN THE SHEEP?

SHOULD I LIMBO UNDER OR JUST KICK IT DOWN?

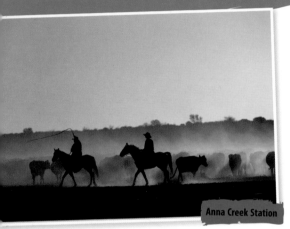

Anna Creek Station

**Size surprise**
Anna Creek in South Australia is a station the size of a nation! It is the biggest working cattle ranch in the world and is about the same size as Belgium.

## FARM ALARM!

In Australia some wild animals are raised on farms, which can cause some alarm.

**Eggs-tremely dangerous**
Keeping crocodiles is not for the fainthearted farmer. Female crocodiles lay about 50 eggs in the nesting season, but one of the trickiest jobs on the farm is collecting the eggs!

**Fence fright**
An emu is a big flightless bird, so this is a bird that you can safely farm knowing that it will not fly over the farm fence. But the emu is not totally defenseless! Its strong legs can kick down a wire fence.

### Parched paddocks
One bad drought was known as the "Big Dry." It affected southeastern Australia and lasted a decade, ending in 2010. But the drama did not end there. Some farmers had to deal with the worst locust plague in 30 years!

> A big ranch in Australia is known as a station.

> I ALWAYS WANTED TO BE A BAA-BAA.

> A cowboy is called a jackaroo. A cowgirl is a jillaroo.

### Milk minders
To survive the drought years, some farmers "cow park." This is when you lend your cows to another farmer to look after them. The only trouble is that the farmer also gets to "look after" their milk!

### Cool in wool?
Australia is the driest inhabited continent on Earth. Surprisingly, wool helps protect sheep from extreme cold and extreme heat. Even so, shearers help sheep beat the heat by cutting away their coats before summer. It sure pays to fleece them!

WANT MORE?

# PAVLOVA ON A PLATE

Australia started a squabble when it claimed the pavlova dessert as its very own. Its neighbor, New Zealand, thought that it was the first to whip up the tasty treat in 1929. But one thing they do agree on is that the cake, made of meringue and topped with lashings of cream and fruit, was named after the Russian ballerina Anna Pavlova, who was as light as air when she danced. There are other stories, too. There have been food fights, food findings, and even food flukes that have led to some tasty tucker.

> I THOUGHT IT WAS BECAUSE THE DESSERT LOOKS LIKE MY TUTU.

Anna Pavlova, 1929

> I'LL FIGHT YOU FOR THOSE BISCUITS.

### Food fight

Australia and New Zealand go into battle over Anzac biscuits, too. These were first sent to the troops fighting in World War I. Anzac stands for Australian and New Zealand Army Corps. No matter who cooked up the first batch, both armies agree that they were far nicer than their usual hardtack biscuits, which some soldiers made into picture frames!

### A ROTTEN START

Some people are nuts about Granny Smith apples, and it's all thanks to Mrs. Maria Smith, also known as Granny Smith. The story goes that in 1868, she threw out some rotten French crab apples. Mysteriously, a new variety of seedling apple took root. Sadly, she did not see the fruits of her labour. She died before the apples became a commercial variety.

### TUCKER TALK

The word "tucker" in Australia means "food." Many Australian foods end up in people's tuckerboxes.

The word "bikkie" is Australian slang for "biscuit."

## The mighty spread

In 1922 an Australian chemist named Dr. Cyril P. Callister invented the famous breakfast spread Vegemite. Labeled "Pure Vegetable Extract," the Vegemite jar found its way onto kitchen tables all over Australia. Today, Vegemite is even sold in containers that look like toothpaste tubes.

VEGEMITE
KRAFT

## What a butterfingers

Legend has it that lamingtons came about thanks to the fumbling fingers of a maid. Named after Lord Lamington, who was Governor of Queensland from 1896 to 1901, these sponge treats, which are dipped in chocolate and coconut, were described by Lord Lamington himself as "poofy woolly biscuits.'"

Lamington

HEY, LOOK, THEY MAKE BLACK TOOTHPASTE NOW!

Anzac biscuits

Pavlova

WANT MORE?

In 1923 a contest was held to name the breakfast spread now called Vegemite.

# THE £10 TICKET

In the 1960s, for just £10, Brits who were under 45 years of age could emigrate to Australia, and kids went for free. When the Ten Pound Pom scheme started in 1947, 400,000 people pounded the pavement to register for the £10 tickets. The Brits were eager to leave behind the rain and rationing to start a new life in the land of sea, surf, and sun. Postwar Australia believed it had to "populate or perish!"

## PRISONERS, POTATOES, AND POMEGRANATES

Here are some different ideas about how the term "Pom" originated:

Pom is short for "prisoner of Mother England" and refers to the convicts who were transported to Australia from the UK from 1787 to 1868.

Australian soldiers called the British troops during World War II "Poms" because the British ate an instant mashed potato called Pom. How s'mashing!

When the Ten Pound Poms arrived, the hot sun made their pale round cheeks turn rosy red, so they looked like pomegranates.

SPELL "EINWANDERUNGSQUOTE."

**Pass the test**
In the 1950s, to qualify for the Ten Pound Pom scheme, adults had to pass a medical examination. Back in 1901, a hopeful immigrant had to write 50 words correctly that the officer dictated. Sounds easy, except the officer could choose 50 words from any language!

Redback spider

## Dangerous dunnies

The Ten Pound Poms found some things in Australia foreign. Many of them had lovely flush toilets back home. Imagine their horror when they saw the Australian "dunny," which was often a dry toilet down the end of the garden. The toilet was called the "thunderbox," and venomous spiders and snakes often went to the loo, too.

WHERE'S SPIDER-MAN WHEN YOU NEED HIM?

## Beating the heat

The Ten Pound Poms almost did perish! They were housed in steel huts in hostels. The huts got so hot in summer that they had to be sprayed with water to cool them down. Some Ten Pound Poms said it was like living in a concentration camp. What a hostile hostel!

THESE HUTS MAKE ME HOT UNDER THE COLLAR!

## There and back

If you throw a boomerang, it comes back. For those Ten Pound Poms who left Australia, went back home, and then returned to Australia, they were given the name Boomerang Poms. There are also Ping-Pong Poms, who go back and forth many times between Australia and home. No wonder they feel homesick!

If you went home within two years of arriving in Australia, you had to pay back £110.

WANT MORE?

Meet some famous Ten Pound Poms ☆ tenpoundpom.com/famous-poms.php

# THE BOXING BOUNCERS

When your family name means "big feet," you are bound to put those feet to good use. Kangaroos use their hind feet to hop, jump, and even box. Male bush bouncers become bush boxers as they fight to see which is the biggest, bravest kangaroo. A boxing match starts with them grabbing each other with their forearms while kicking with their large back legs. Boxing kangaroos have come to symbolize the fighting spirit of Australians, particularly those who battle it out in the sporting arena.

### Boxed around the ears

In 2011 a 94-year-old woman in Queensland showed her fighting spirit when a rogue red kangaroo decided to go into battle with her as she hung out her laundry. Luckily, the woman was able to arm herself with a nearby broom. She tried to give the roo the brush-off by bopping it on its head. When that didn't work, the woman crawled to safety!

QUICK, HIDE IN HERE.

Australia's national soccer team is nicknamed the Socceroos.

# 1 SIZING THEM UP

There are 61 species in the kangaroo family, but the biggest of them all is the red kangaroo.

Check out these facts:

- ✫ largest living marsupial
- ✫ male stands about 6ft (1.8m) high
- ✫ hind feet can be 18in (45cm) long
- ✫ tail can be 35in (90cm) long
- ✫ can cover 26ft (8m) in a single leap
- ✫ baby the size of a jellybean at birth

I'D RATHER BOUNCE THAN BOX.

### Roo in the ring

One kangaroo ended up in real boxing bouts in 1891. Mrs. Olivia Mayne bought "Fighting Jack" for £1 and taught him to box. But she had a fight on her hands when the theater owners refused to pay her fee when Jack refused to box.

## A SPORTING SPIRIT

At any Australian sporting event, you are likely to see mobs of kangaroos. There might be giant inflatable kangaroos, toy kangaroos on top of people's hats, or even fans dressed up as kangaroos. But one of the most patriotic kangaroos of all is a boxing kangaroo named BK. It is Australia's official Olympic mascot. What a sport!

### Kangaroos go into battle

During World War II (1939–45), the Australian Air Force painted kangaroos—sometimes boxing kangaroos—onto the sides of their planes. When an Australian pilot "knocked out" an enemy plane, a cross was added to his plane.

WANT MORE?

Fun facts ✫ www.dfat.gov.au/facts/kangaroos.html

# HOME OF THE HOIST

Always being miles away from anywhere else made Australians head off to their sheds to whip up what they did not have. One such inventor was Lance Hill. In his backyard in 1945, he created a clothesline from next to nothing. Hill's wife had simply asked him to make a clothesline that did not get in the way of her lemon tree. He did just that, and his invention was no lemon. Selling his "metal trees," or Hills Hoists, which hoisted the clothes and spun them around, was simply a breeze!

### Homespun fun!

In every great Australian backyard, there is one piece of equipment that children still love to play on—the Hills Hoist. However, the clothesline's instruction manual strongly advises that children (and pets!) do not swing on it. Talk about getting them into line.

I FEEL PEGGED OUT!

### Queen of clotheslines

In 1959 the Hills company thought that its clothesline was the perfect present for the Queen and her mother. But that got the Governor-General, Sir William Slim, in a real spin. He didn't think it was a suitable gift to send to the royal palace. So she never got to be the queen of clean!

I'M GOING INTO A TAILSPIN...

During Cyclone Tracy in 1974, the only thing left on one property was the Hills Hoist.

# BACKYARD BRAINWAVES

The great Aussie backyard is buzzing with activity and great ideas.

## Utes are beauts
Coupe utility cars, or utes, first rolled into backyards in 1934, thanks to a farmer's wife who was tired of going to church in a farm truck and arriving looking like a pigsty! She wanted a car that could take her to church on Sunday and the pigs to market on Monday.

## Suds and subs
The first Hills Hoist was made from metal tubing that had once been part of an underwater boom under the Sydney Harbour Bridge. The boom was there to snag any enemy submarines!

## Grassroot inventors
In 1948 Lawrence Hall built a rotary-blade lawn mower with a steel frame and a boat motor. It was so heavy that Hall's son and nephew had to drag it along with a rope. So Mervyn Victor Richardson, who had seen Hall's mower four years earlier, came up with a lightweight mower. The fuel tank was a peach tin. He named his creation Victa.

WANT MORE?

# FOOTY MaD!

If you think Roman gladiators were hard nuts, meet the muscle-shirted maestros of Australian football, or "Aussie rules." Australia's favorite game is a mad mix of rugby, basketball, and professional wrestling! The matches are thrilling, the crowds enormous, and the rivalries fierce, especially in the sport's home state of Victoria. And it's not just for men. There are females playing in teams all over Australia.

**On your marks!**
When a player catches a kicked ball cleanly, it's called a mark. The big crowd-pleasers are the high-flying spectacular marks, or "speckies." At the end of each season, the best mark is honored with the Mark of the Year award.

I CAN SEE THE SYDNEY OPERA HOUSE FROM UP HERE.

THAT'S A BIT OVER THE TOP!

## Footy kicks off

Aussie rules comes from Melbourne, Victoria. It began in the 1850s as a way of keeping cricketers fit in the off-season. One early game lasted three days, had forty players on each team, and a pitch 2,625ft (800m) long!

## Heavy hitters

The white-coated umpires with their strange hand gestures are a distinctive feature of footy. But spare a thought for the unfortunately named Ivor Crapp. Known in his day as the "Prince of Umpires," Crapp was attacked more than once by furious fans.

> THESE PILLOWCASES SHOULD DRY IN NO TIME!

50

## FOOTY FACTS

The playing field is oval and has four goalposts at each end.

Each team has 22 players, with 18 allowed on the field at one time.

The ball must be kicked or punched; throwing is illegal.

A player running with the ball must bounce it every few meters.

A goal is scored by kicking the ball between the "big sticks."

An umpire returns the ball into play by throwing it backward!

## Farewell finger

When Brett Backwell's broken finger threatened to cut short his Aussie rules career, he had the finger cut off instead! Amazingly, the next year, he won South Australia's top player award, the Magarey Medal.

> WILL IT BE YOUR FINGER OR FOOTY TODAY?

WANT MORE?

**Australian Football League official site** ☆ www.afl.com.au

THAT WAS HIS BEST SHIRT, TOO!

## MR. AND MRS. BUSHRANGER

Frederick Ward became Captain Thunderbolt when a clap of thunder cracked violently as he banged on the door of some poor victims. Mrs. Thunderbolt, or Mary Ann Bugg, is believed to have helped her husband and his mate escape from the prison on Cockatoo Island. In 1870 Captain Thunderbolt got a real bolt from the blue when he was shot dead by a pursuing policeman.

### As rotten as eggs

Dan "Mad Dog" Morgan, always fearing people were out to poison him, swiped only boiled eggs when he robbed people's pantries. When he died, he got himself in a real pickle. His head was preserved in a jar of vinegar and sent to Melbourne University— or is that Smellbourne University?

WHAT AN EGGHEAD.

A dead Dan Morgan

### From bad stealer to bad speller

George Scott, aka Captain Moonlite, turned from preacher to pillager when he robbed a bank in 1869. But he had some bad luck. The bank manager knew him. Captain Moonlite wrote a note to say that the manager had been forced to hand over the loot. That's when a writing crime took place—he couldn't spell "Moonlight."

Moonlite

# BUSHRANGER BADDIES

When convict crims busted out of jail and bolted into the bush, they instantly began life as a bushranger. These "bolters," or bush bandits, either lived off the land or simply robbed for a living. Not all bushrangers were convicts. Sometimes young men just took to the bush to escape the drudgery of everyday life. But some bushrangers were mad, and some were just downright bad. For many of these looters and shooters, their days in the bush ended with a policeman's bullet or on the end of a dangling rope.

Ned Devine

Ned's coach and horses

MY NAME'S RED, NED!

## Dead famous

John Whitehead and his band of bushrangers were real bullies. They made one police informer put on shoes teeming with bull ants. The man died a dastardly death. But Whitehead had a more gruesome end. He asked his bushranger buddy, Michael Howe, to cut off his head and hide it before the soldiers captured him. The head was hidden inside a hanky!

IT'S BETTER THAN ANTS IN YOUR PANTS!

## A jolly good joker

Where there are bushrangers, there are stagecoaches. Ned Devine was a coach driver who liked to play practical jokes. Once he told his passengers he had trained a kangaroo to greet the coach, grab the mail, and deliver it. Imagine the passengers' surprise when Ned shot around a corner and yelled to some random roo by the road, "Nothing for you today, Jack!"

WANT MORE?

# A SEA VIEW

Captain James Cook was one of the first Europeans to see the Great Barrier Reef, but he could not really avoid it—his ship ran aground on the reef on June 11, 1770. There was probably no time to admire the beauty, as those aboard had to throw out anything that was heavy, including the cannon, to help refloat the ship. But if they had paused a moment, they would have seen some of the most colorful fish in the world. Luckily, today's explorers can see the dazzling sights through the safety of a glass-bottomed boat.

**Sightseeing from space**
When astronauts first explored space, one of the wonders that they saw out the spacecraft window was the Great Barrier Reef. It is the largest living structure on our planet. Far out!

THIS PLACE HAS A GREAT SEA VIEW.

**Loud and clear**
Some creatures are seen and heard. The pistol shrimp is small, but its claw creates a real commotion in the ocean. When it snaps its claw shut, the sound is louder than a jet engine. The shock wave it sends out stuns its prey.

There are about 30 shipwrecks on the Great Barrier Reef.

# DANGEROUS BEAUTY

It is best to see some creatures on the Great Barrier Reef before they see you.

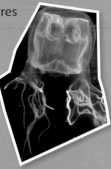

☆ The box jellyfish is not a box of fun! You are not likely to survive its sting. Keep an eye out for it— it looks like a box.

> IS THAT A BOX OR A JELLYFISH?

☆ The blue-ringed octopus must grab you with its eight tentacles in order to bite you. So watch out, it is armed and dangerous.

Dead coral

**A skeleton reef**
In water, corals are brilliant colors, such as red, purple, blue, green, and yellow. But if you take them out of the water, they die and turn white. Coral "skeletons" form coral reefs. So coral reefs are deadly!

Sometimes crocodiles swim in the Great Barrier Reef!

NO VACANCIES

**Unseen but unclean**
Not all creatures like to be seen. Hiding is one way of keeping safe on the reef. The pearl fish has an unusual hiding place—in a sea cucumber's bottom. It might be worse for the sea cucumber though, because pearl fish often live in pairs!

WANT MORE?

Great Barrier Reef Marine Park Authority ☆ www.gbrmpa.gov.au

# CUTE AND CUDDLY?

Koalas are fuzzy furballs that lead a lazy life. They sleep, sleep, and then sleep some more, and when they are not slumbering and snoozing during the day and for much of the night, they are munching on leaves. Koalas are not only fuzzy, they are fussy, too. They usually eat only eucalyptus leaves, and so when they are Australia's ambassadors living in a zoo that is far away from any eucalyptus trees, there is an express delivery of branches to them twice a week. Now that's room service!

PITY I CAN'T EAT IN MY SLEEP.

I AM NOT KOALA POOP, SO PLEASE DON'T EAT ME.

**The scoop on poop**
Fancy bullet-shaped koala poop dangling from your ears? One company definitely had the motto "waste not, want not" and decided that koala poop would make lovely earrings. Mind you, it might not be so bad. Koala poop can have a eucalyptus odor. However, it would be a case of "first in, best dressed" because young koalas eat their mother's poop!

Koalas sleep for about 20 hours a day.

## A wee warning

You can't be cute and cuddly all the time. To stamp their mark on their territory, males rub their chests on tree trunks and leave behind a dark, sticky substance. It is a koala calling card that means, "Back off, buddy." To scare away other animals, koalas often just urinate on them!

It is illegal to have a pet koala.

THIS IS YOUR LAST WARNING!

### EAT YOUR HEART OUT

Koalas are picky eaters. They eat mainly the leaves and young shoots of the eucalyptus tree. There are about 600 different kinds of eucalyptus trees. Koalas eat the leaves of about 120 of them, but they prefer only about 6.

### Pardon me!

Male koalas make a loud snoring sound, and that's when they are awake! During the breeding season, males try to attract a female with loud bellows that sound a bit like loud snores. To top it off, they then make belching noises. How unattractive.

NO KOALA WAS HARMED IN THE MAKING OF THIS BAG.

### A fur fight

Some people thought that koalas were so cute that they just had to wear them. In Queensland in 1927, about 800,000 koala skins were traded in just one month. That really made the fur fly! Luckily, the fashion police soon stepped in. Killing koalas became illegal by 1937.

WANT MORE?

**Australian Koala Foundation** ☆ www.savethekoala.com

# FELONS NOT FARMERS

In the early days of settlement, life for the crims was grim, and it wasn't all peaches and cream for the non-convicts either. The British might have brought enough stuff to almost sink a ship, but it didn't last long. When food supplies ran low or rotted, Governor Arthur Phillip reduced everyone's food rations. He also gave the convicts Saturday afternoons off so that they could grow their own food. Rations were so low even the Governor's dinner guests had to bring their own bread!

Governor Arthur Phillip

### Enough stuff?
The First Fleet needed to carry supplies not only for the journey, but also to set up a colony once it arrived in Australia. The supplies included 700 garden hoes, 700 shovels, 40 wheelbarrows, and, most important of all, 250 handkerchiefs. After all, the convicts had plenty to cry about!

## CONVICT KIDS

Not all the convicts were adults, and it is just as well because the child convicts ate less.

**Mary Wade—11 years old:** She was sentenced to hang for attacking an eight-year-old girl for her cotton frock, a linen hat, and a linen shawl, but in the end, Mary was sent to Australia for life.

**John Hudson—12 years old:** Because he was a chimney sweep, he had access to people's houses. He stole a linen shirt, two aprons, five silk stockings, and a pistol. He got a seven-year sentence to Australia.

### Food fight
Most of the convicts had light fingers—not green fingers. Many crops failed in the first year, so food rations were cut further. This made the soldiers grumble as loudly as their stomachs. They got the same amount as the convicts.

## Garden greens
Governor Phillip set up a vegetable garden on this island in Sydney Harbour. It became known as Garden Island.

## No guardian angel
In 1789 HMS *Guardian* set sail for the new colony with supplies. However, she hit an iceberg. To stop the ship from sinking, cargo, guns, and cattle were thrown overboard. But the crew saved 2,380 gallons (9,000 L) of wine to help them drown their sorrows!

ANYONE FOR ICE WITH THEIR WINE?

## Steal or starve
Starvation was a real problem in the early days, and so was stealing food. One convict got 500 lashes (not lashings) for stealing a pumpkin. In 1789 six marines were hanged for swiping food from the government stores. It didn't pay to steal a meal!

One convict ate his week's food rations all at once. He died the next day.

## Jailbirds!
Cockatoo Island was established as a convict prison in 1839. The island was named after the huge flock of cockatoos that lived there. However, the birds took off once the convicts arrived. Not surprising really. Convicts were known to eat wombats, emus, kangaroos, and cockatoos.

POLLY WANTS A CRACKER!

## The veggie villain
Convicts did not receive rations of fresh vegetables and fruit, so John "Black" Caesar just helped himself. When he was captured after escaping into the bush, he was made to work in the vegetable gardens at Garden Island. He made sure he ate his veggies!

WANT MORE?

Cockatoo Island in Sydney Harbour  ☆ www.cockatooisland.gov.au

# BUSHFIRE!

Imagine the air being so hot from a bushfire that birds and bats just fall out of the sky. Australia is the most fire-prone continent on the planet. For animals that survive a raging inferno, there is hope and help on hand, and people are touched by these bush battlers' survival stories. The ultimate survivors are termites. Bushfires sweep over termite mounds but the mounds are well insulated from the scorching heat, so the termite colony lives on. What lucky little firefighters!

I'M NOT "FRILLED" ABOUT FIRES!

## The face of fire

The frilled-neck lizard is one of the faces of fire prevention campaigns. However, not all fires are preventable because natural events, such as lightning, can start them. But if a frilled-neck lizard survives a fire, it can often eat double its usual intake. Its food—insects, termites, and centipedes—have no place to hide.

*Fires usually move faster up a hill and slower down a hill.*

## Thirst to survive

Suffering from burns and thirst, Sam the koala took a drink from a firefighter's water bottle after a fire in 2009. A photo of this courageous koala spread like wildfire around the world.

Sam the koala

We like our lizards frilled NOT grilled

BUSHFIRES COUNCIL N.T.

*DO YOU WANT TO BORROW MY BURROW?*

## Digging deep

Wombats have the perfect fire escape. They hide in their burrows under the ground until the flames have passed overhead. But their fight for survival usually begins after the flames have died down. They feed on vegetation, such as grasses, and they don't like it chargrilled!

*Seedlings grow in the beds of ash.*

## ANIMALS TO THE RESCUE

In 2012 an Australian scientist suggested a drastic fire plan. He thought that grazers, such as elephants and rhinos, could be introduced into Australia to eat the flammable grasses. Another scientist agreed that the elephants could help reduce fire risks, but there was a drawback —they would increase the risks to humans!

WANT MORE?

**Australia's two deadliest bushfires are known as Ash Wednesday and Black Saturday.**

Ophidiophobia
is the fear
of snakes.

AHH—I'M
SCARED OF
SNAKES!

Western brown snake

### S-s-s-seriously scary

Australians have an old saying: "as mad as a cut snake." Whoever coined it must have had the brown snake in mind. Brown snakes win the title of Australia's most irritable reptile. If disturbed, they like nothing better than a quick game of "chase and chomp." Even though their fangs are tiny, brown snakes kill more Australians than any other snake.

# SNAKE PHOBIA!

Australia is home to the biggest collection of surly serpents, rancid reptiles, and venomous vipers on the planet. In fact, the top ten venomous snakes on Earth call Australia home. The good news is that snakes are usually too busy minding their own business to bother people. And if they do bite, antivenins are close at hand. The bad news is that there is still no cure for snake phobia!

A 30ft (9m) long snake roamed Queensland
about 4.5 million years ago.

# TOP TEN DEADLY LAND SNAKES

1. Inland taipan
2. Eastern brown snake
3. Coastal taipan
4. Tiger snake
5. Black tiger snake
6. Black tiger snake (yes, there are two different kinds!)
7. Death adder
8. Western brown snake
9. Spotted brown snake
10. Australian copperhead

## A mouse murderer

The inland taipan enjoys the quiet life in the desert. But its fangs are locked and loaded with the snake world's most potent ammunition. One bite has enough venom to polish off a quarter of a million mice. Now that's overkill!

## Not-so-nice neighbors

In 2011 hundreds of snakes filled the flooded streets of Rockhampton, Queensland. Many locals were trapped in their houses by the rising water. They did not take kindly to having wet, cranky snakes climbing inside to dry off!

## MILKING TIME

Snake venoms are toxic cocktails, and each snake has its own special recipe. If you get bitten, you need to be given the right antivenin for that snake. To make antivenins, snakes are carefully "milked." It's just like milking a cow, except that a snake's "milk" can kill you!

> THIS GLASS IS HISSSS-TORY!

## Super snake

Atomic Betty is the biggest snake in Australia. When Betty lost her slender shape, her zookeepers put her on a crash diet. Poor Betty was allowed to eat only three or four goats a year!

WANT MORE?

**Australian Museum** ☆ www.australianmuseum.net.au/Australian-Snakes

# DREAMTIME

Australian Indigenous culture is based in the spiritual beliefs and stories called the "Dreaming." Each place and its people have a different Dreaming, but it always begins with the Dreamtime. This was the time of Creation when giant Ancestral Beings formed themselves, the world, and its laws. They journeyed far and wide, molding the landscape and giving rise to the people and animals. Aboriginal people had no written language, so the Dreaming was passed from old to young through dance, music, and art.

## MEET THE ANCESTORS

★ **Baiame**, the Sky Father, came down to Earth to create mountains and forests, and to educate the people.

★ Baiame's wife was the emu, **Birrangulu**, and their son was **Daramulum**, who speaks through the whirling instrument, the bullroarer.

★ The **Rainbow Serpent** was a giant snake, who burst from Earth to create rivers and streams. He dwells in the deepest water holes.

**ART ROCKS!**

### Dreamtime designs
It was 1891, and Joseph Bradshaw was lost. He was looking for some land he had bought in the remote Kimberley region of Western Australia. Instead, he found astonishing pictures that seemed as ancient as the rock walls they were painted on. The local people call the pictures "Gwion Gwion," after the Dreamtime Being who created them.

## Songs of the desert

"Songlines" are the routes followed by Ancestral Beings in their Dreamtime journeys across the land. Landmarks and sacred places were recorded in songs. In the days before GPS, songlines were the safest way to get across the desert—as long as you didn't get the words mixed up!

Devils Marbles, Northern Territory

## Dance party

A corroboree is an Indigenous dance party. At these ceremonial occasions, the Dreamtime is sung and danced from one generation to the next. At a corroboree, watching your dad dance isn't embarrassing, it's educational!

YIKES, I'M EVEN SCARING MYSELF!

## Dotted lines

Aboriginal paintings tell stories from the Dreaming, painstakingly depicted with dots and flat, stylized shapes. Art lovers go dotty over these mystical masterpieces!

## BEWARE THE BUNYIP

Aboriginal mythology tells of a dank and devilish creature called the bunyip, which lurks in rivers and swamps. Nobody is quite sure what it looks like, but that hasn't stopped people from claiming to have seen it. It has even been suggested that the boggy beast is based on an extinct giant wombat.

WANT MORE?

Explore the animated world of the Dreamtime ☆ www.abc.net.au/dustechoes

# HAIL THE BAGGY GREENS!

The words "Australia" and "cricket" mean the same to many people. Australians love to see the national team in their "baggy green" caps celebrating yet another victory. But, as famous as today's zinc-painted wicket warriors are, Australia's greatest cricketing hero came from a very different time. Sir Donald Bradman was one of the finest players who ever swung a bat. When England's cricketers tried to stop him, the result was often all-out war!

### Top hat
The famous "baggy green" cap is given to new players on their debut for the Australian Test team. A clapped-out old cap is a mark of seniority. Maybe they should look after them better—this one belonged to Sir Donald Bradman and sold at auction for A$425,000!

Sir Donald Bradman

### Body on the line
The English team thought they had figured out how to stop Bradman scoring. They battered him and his teammates with bruising bouncers aimed at the head and body. This "bodyline" tactic won them the 1932–33 Ashes, but it created such a stink that the rules were changed to stop it happening again!

### 'The Don'
The great Australian batsman Sir Donald Bradman terrorized opponents in the 1930s and 1940s. As a boy, he taught himself to play by hitting a golf ball against a water tank with a cricket stump. "The Don'"retired with a batting average of almost 100.

## BEST ENEMIES

The rivalry between Australia and England is the oldest in cricket. It is symbolized by a small urn of ashes. Nobody is quite sure what the ashes are from. Perhaps they are the ashes of England's cricketing pride, since, over the years, Australia has often got the better of its old rival.

**Girls on the green**
The Southern Stars are Australia's women's team. Not to be outdone by their male counterparts, they have won more World Cups than any other team. What superstars!

STOP MUCKING ABOUT. THIS IS A TEST!

THESE BOXING GLOVES ARE A NUISANCE.

**What a sport**
Former Australian team captain Mark Taylor once stopped batting when he had 334 runs. He did not want to beat Sir Don Bradman's highest Test score!

WANT MORE?

Cricket terms and sayings ☆ www.wandererscricket.com/glossary.html

# BUSH TUCKER

The Australian bush is where Australian legends were made; where people pitted themselves against the elements while waiting for the "billy to boil." The bush is often a dry, sparse place. But if you know where to look, it is a richly stocked pantry. Australians call wild foods "bush tucker." From kangaroos to caterpillars, goannas to bush bananas—don't be shy, tuck in!

## How to cook a galah
Here is one of many joke recipes for cooking this tough bird. Put a galah in a pot of water with herbs and three rocks. Bring this to the boil and simmer for a few hours. When the rocks are tender, throw away the galah, and eat the rocks!

> DO YOU WANT FLIES WITH THAT?

> Do the "Aussie salute"-- wave your hands around so you don't accidentally swallow a fly!

## Bush icon
The leaves of some eucalyptus, or gum trees, are used to make eucalyptus oil. This is what gives cough drops and antiseptic creams that distinctive taste and smell. A gum leaf can also be added to a billy of tea for that real bush flavor. Just don't add milk!

> WITCHETTY ONE OF US LOOKS THE YUMMIEST?

## Grub's up!
Mmmm, what could be nicer than a yummy, nutty witchetty grub, wriggling and writhing? You can eat them cooked or raw. They are very nutritious and taste like eggs. Or so they say!

**Bush kitchen rules!**
Some bush foods, such
as lemon myrtle and
kangaroo meat, can already
be found in supermarkets
and on restaurant menus.
Echidna enchiladas may
take a bit longer.

EAT *THEM.*
I'M SMALL FRY!

WANT
MORE?

**For a great bush-tucker fact sheet** ☆ **www.wettropics.gov.au/st/st_facts.html**

# A ROUGH RaCE

The Sydney Hobart Yacht Race is no picnic. But plenty of people armed with picnics go to watch the yachts set sail from Sydney Harbour on Boxing Day (December 26). It pays to pack plenty of Christmas leftovers in your picnic basket. The winner of the first race in 1945 finished after 6 days, 14 hours, and 22 minutes. As for the sailors, there really is no time to nibble on turkey drumsticks. The race is only for hardy sailors, or maybe just foolhardy ones. Some sailors reckon that it would be more pleasant to take a cold shower and be beaten with a cricket bat!

## No adults, please

This ocean race is not just for salty old sea dogs. Jessica Watson, who in 2010 was the youngest person to sail solo and unassisted around the world, skippered a yacht in the 2011 race. It was not all plain sailing though. She was hit in the face by a flying fish!

The first woman to cross the finish line was Jane Tate in 1946.

Jessica Watson

## Farewell flotilla

There is much commotion on the ocean on race day, and that is just from the spectators. Hundreds of spectator boats farewell the racing yachts. In 1971, a car even took to the water. Luckily, it was an amphibious car, so it could float like a boat!

**Towering waves**

The race's nickname, "hell on high water," suggests high drama on the high seas. In 1998, when a "weather bomb" hit the race, no one knew that the waves would tower eight stories high. Tragically, five boats sank and six sailors died. A further 55 sailors were rescued.

SYDNEY

Just nine boats took part in the very first race.

BASS STRAIT

IS THAT A WAVE OR A WHALE SPOUT?

**Strait talking**

Bass Strait is known as "the paddock." But sailors know the fury of this patch of ocean. The sea can be dead calm and glassy (not grassy!) one minute and then just plain deadly the next.

HOBART

# RECORD BREAKERS

★ **Closest finish**
In 2001 the first six boats all finished within 47 minutes of each other.

★ **Slowest race**
*Wayfarer*, in 1945, completed the course in 11 days, 6 hours, and 20 minutes.

★ **Fastest race**
*Wild Oats* took out the honour in 2005, with a time of 1 day, 18 hours, and 40 minutes.

★ **Oldest skipper**
The young-at-heart John Walker was 86 when he raced in 2008.

WANT MORE?

**Sydney Hobart Yacht Race official site** ★ www.rolexsydneyhobart.com

# WALTZING MATILDA

It would be easy if you didn't know the song to think that "Waltzing Matilda" was about a girl named Matilda who liked to waltz. But this famous bush ballad tells a tragic tale of a swagman who, after being tracked down by three troopers for stealing a jumbuck, throws himself into a billabong and drowns. The story behind the song begins with A.B. Paterson, a bush poet who usually signed his name "The Banjo." But a woman named Christina Macpherson should also take a spot in the limelight.

### Tuned into tea
A billy was a swagman's best mate. It doubled as a cooking pot and kettle. It is not surprising then that the swagman in the first verse of the song watched and waited while his billy boiled.

### Singing like billy-oh
Sometimes it's good to change your tune, and that's what happened to the song in 1903. A tea company used the song "Waltzing Matilda" to help promote its product, Billy Tea. It wrapped a copy of the song around each tea packet, although the song was slightly different from the original. Which word got more of a mention? Billy, of course!

MY BEARD LOOKS LIKE A BUSH!

A swag

A billy

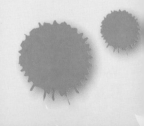

Oh there once was a swagman camped in the billabong,
Under the shade of a Coolibah tree;
And he sang as he looked at the old billy boiling,
Who'll come a-waltzing Matilda with me.

*Original lyrics*

THAT'S STRAIGHT FROM THE HORSE'S MOUTH.

## SONG WORDS

**billabong**—a stagnant part of a river

**billy**—a tin can for making tea

**jumbuck**—a sheep

**swag**—personal belongings

**swagman**—a traveler or a shearer

**trooper**—a cavalry soldier

**waltzing matilda**—to tramp the roads carrying a swag

### A horse, of course
The initials "A.B.P." should really stand for 'A Bush Poet'. But they stand for Andrew Barton Paterson. The solicitor and poet wrote under the pen name "The Banjo," the name of a horse his family owned. To the average bloke, the man is simply known as Banjo Paterson.

"Waltzing Matilda" is the official unofficial national anthem.

HANDS UP!

A sculpture in Winton of the three troopers' revolvers

A zither

### Play it again
In early 1895 Christina Macpherson played from memory the tune of a Scottish march song, called Craigielee, on the zither. She played in the sitting room at Dagworth Station, her family's property near Winton in Queensland. Banjo Paterson was there, too (no, he wasn't playing the banjo) and wrote the words for the first verse, turning it from a Scottish song into a bush ballad. In 1900 Banjo Paterson sold the rights to the song for five pounds!

WANT MORE?

**Listen to "Waltzing Matilda"** ☆ www.nla.gov.au/epubs/waltzingmatilda

# DEADLY NIPPERS

Australians are famous for being warm-hearted and friendly.
But there are some Australians who are cold-blooded and solitary.
They lurk in dark corners with murder in their hearts. They have eight
legs and fangs dripping with venom. They are spiders!
Australia is home to about 2,000 spider species—
from bird-eating spiders to spiders that look like
bird droppings. Only a handful are harmful,
but some of those can kill. So watch out,
and don't forget your shoes!

Wolf spider

## Wolf them down

Meet the big, bad wolf—wolf spider,
that is. Oh my, what big eyes it has.
Wolf spiders have eyes like night-vision
goggles—all the better to see dinner
with after dark!

## Social climber

The Sydney funnel-web
spider has a taste for the
high life. It prefers to live
in Sydney's leafy suburbs.
But don't invite it to your
next dinner party, or you
might end up on the menu.
The male Sydney funnel-web
has a deadly bite!

The Sydney funnel-web
spider is one of the three
most dangerous spiders
in the world.

## Car alarm

Huntsman spiders like to scuttle about inside vehicles. One way to persuade your passenger to leave is to park the vehicle in the sun. The hot huntsman will crawl out an open window. But don't open the window too much, or a car thief might crawl in!

*Redback spider*

*Huntsman spider*

**THESE BOOTS WERE MADE FOR LURKING...**

## Spider survivor

An antivenin for the bite of the Sydney funnel-web spider was finally approved in 1981. It was just in time for Gordon Wheatley. He was bitten on the foot 30 days later and became the miracle drug's first-ever success story.

## TOP OF THE POPS

*There was a redback on the toilet seat,*
*When I was there last night,*
*I didn't see him in the dark,*
*But boy! I felt his bite!*

Country singer Slim Newton had a big hit with his novelty song "Redback on the Toilet Seat." But the redback's bite is no laughing matter—it can be a real bummer!

**I HAVE A RED BACK, TOO!**

## Does it or doesn't it?

The white-tailed spider is the subject of a scientific whodunnit! Some people think the spider's venom causes flesh to rot. Others believe the culprits may be germs on the spider's fangs.

*White-tailed spider*

*Mouse spider*

## Unwelcome guests

In 2001 hundreds of big, venomous mouse spiders invaded a family's backyard in Newcastle, NSW. When they would not leave, the whole lawn was dug up and carted away—hairy intruders and all!

**WANT MORE?**

East Alligator floodplains

Kakadu wetlands

# WiLD, WiLD WET

The Australian outback is all desert, right? Wrong! Kakadu National Park—in Australia's remote far north and covering an area half the size of Switzerland—is a place that plays by its own rules. The landscape is shaped by water. Its weather is so wild it needs six seasons to encompass it, and it houses the biggest outdoor art collection in Australia.

### Thunder Down Under
Here is a striking fact—Kakadu has more lightning than any other place on Earth. During the monsoon season of Gudjewg, the rain sluices down and the lightning crackles for hours each day. According to the locals, lightning is created by Namarrgon. He manages it by having air-splitting axes mounted to his knees and head!

## EXTRA SEASONING

Kakadu has six seasons:

★ **Gudjewg:** wet and wild, with thunderstorms and floods

★ **Banggerreng:** "knock 'em down" storm season— expect high winds

★ **Yegge:** cool and misty

★ **Wurrgeng:** cold—"only" 86°F (30°C)!

★ **Gurrung:** hot and dry

★ **Gunumeleng:** hot and humid, with thunderstorms starting again, and the chance of tropical cyclones

Kakadu has three Alligator Rivers, but no alligators!

*Jim Jim Falls*

## Big bird
Kakadu is home to about one third of Australian bird species. The jabiru, or the black-billed stork, is Australia's largest wading bird. The biggest township in Kakadu is also called Jabiru. That's more than a big coincidence!

## Dexterous dingo
Dingoes are part of Kakadu's wildlife. One special feature of the dingo is that its wrist can rotate easily. This means it can use its paw like a hand and could turn a doorknob. So don't forget to lock the door!

*Rock art at Nanguluwur*

THEY NAMED A TOWN AFTER ME!

*Jabiru*

SHAKE HANDS?

## Art history
Indigenous artists have been leaving their mark on Kakadu's rocks for thousands of years, and they have never stopped. There are ships and World War II planes beside extinct animals and ancient Dreamtime figures.

WANT MORE?

Kakadu National Park ✫ www.environment.gov.au/parks/kakadu

# A WOMAN WITH WINGS

Nancy Bird wanted to fly like a bird. At age four, she attempted her first flight by jumping off the back fence. Growing up in the pioneering days of flight, Nancy Bird was a pioneer herself, becoming the youngest woman to gain a commercial pilot's license. In 1933, it was unusual for a woman to fly, and just as unusual for them to wear trousers when they did so. But Nancy Bird was made of tough stuff. Navigating with just a compass, a watch, and a road map, she often had to fly by the seat of her pants!

## Wings and wood
To earn a living, Nancy Bird used to take people on joy flights at fairs. Her copilot would spin the propeller, sell the tickets, and make sure the passengers did not put their feet through the wings. The wings were made from wood and fabric, and were stuck together with glue.

Peggy McKillop · Nancy Bird

## The flying birds

Nancy Bird was like a little bird. When she started to fly, she had to sit on a large cushion to see out of the cockpit and reach the plane's pedals! Her copilot, Peggy McKillop, sometimes wore a padded flying suit, so the flying duo were nicknamed "Little Bird" and "Big Bird."

## Mercy Dash

Known as "the Angel of the Outback," Nancy often dashed to pick up sick people who lived days from medical help. Nancy also flew people and supplies across the vast continent. Once she had a very urgent delivery—she flew ice cream to a picnic!

Nancy would often tie her plane to a fence at night to stop it from blowing away.

### Landmark flying

In the early days of flying, there were usually no aviation maps. A pilot would search for familiar landmarks, such as railroad tracks or even wheel tracks. One time, a pilot who flew a mail service told Nancy about an unusual landmark. It was a dead horse, and he said you could smell it from up in the air!

WHEN I WENT TO HEAVEN, I GOT WINGS, TOO!

### A trailblazer

Nancy took on all kinds of flying jobs in order to be able to afford gas for her plane. In the 1930s, the editor of a newspaper paid Nancy to hang a sign with the word "Woman" from her plane to advertise a new magazine.

WOMAN

## BUNNY-HOP LANDINGS

A landing strip in Nancy's day was often a farm field. Nancy would make the farmer drive a car quickly across the field. She could tell how suitable the field was for landing by how much the car bounced along. Rabbit holes made a car bunny hop badly!

WANT MORE?

First Lady of Aviation ☆ www.australianbiography.gov.au/subjects/birdwalton

# A Town Named Alice

Alice Springs, the town that people fondly call "Alice," started out with the name Stuart! This famous outback town is the heart and soul of Australia's interior. Early explorers called the interior "the dead heart" because the red soil looked like blood and the vast, barren land seemed lifeless. But when the telegraph came to town in 1872, the town of the Red Center became the center of attention.

## Stuart the Scotsman

The town of Stuart was named after the Scottish explorer John McDouall Stuart, who probably felt like he had a dead heart at times. He set out in October 1861 to find a route for an overland telegraph line across Australia from south to north. After much hardship, Stuart succeeded in July 1862. Although at times he was too weak to walk!

**John McDouall Stuart**

The town Stuart became Alice Springs in 1933.

## End of the line

During the 1940s Alice Springs was the end of the line. The railway line from Adelaide ended there. During World War II, Alice Springs became a gathering point for troops heading north to Darwin. The troops went by truck to Darwin, and at first, the drivers navigated their way by following the wire of the Overland Telegraph!

IT'S A MESSAGE FOR SOMEONE NAMED ALICE.

**Telegraph station, Alice Springs**

## Crank up the camels

Camels were once used as pack animals for the construction of the telegraph line. Now they are the stars of the Camel Cup, which all started because of a bet between two friends at a pub in 1970. You can bet the camels wished it hadn't!

## Alice who?

Alice Springs was named after a real Alice, but her surname was not Springs. Alice was the wife of the Postmaster General of South Australia, Sir Charles Todd. The "Springs" in the township's name is thanks to a water hole that is a short distance east of the telegraph station buildings.

THIS IS DEFINITELY A SANDY SHORE!

## SAND SAILORS

This race deserves all the attention it gets. What other place holds a boat race when the nearest body of water is 930mi (1,500km) away? The Henley-on-Todd Regatta takes place on the dry, sandy Todd River. In fact, water is not welcome. The race is cancelled if the river has water in it!

WANT MORE?

History, news, and events ☆ www.alicesprings.nt.gov.au

# BEACH BANS

Today, the sea, surf, and sand are free, but back in the early 1900s there was little freedom at the beach. There were rules about who you could swim with and what you could swim in. Alexander MacRae had a manufacturing business that first started making swimwear in 1914. The name of his swimwear was "Fortitude," and fortitude is what he needed when some of his beachwear was banned! Luckily, by the 1960s, the restrictive rules and regulations started to relax, and people could finally enjoy the freedom that the beaches offered.

**IS THE COAST CLEAR?**

**The not-seen scene**
In the 1920s, beach-goers were not keen on being seen. They would duck into a bathing box to cover themselves up with their neck-to-knee swimsuits. Some bathing boxes had wheels, so people could be rolled down the beach and even into the water!

**I MISS MY WHEELS.**

**SHE LOOKS LIKE A FISH OUT OF WATER.**

In 1907, three mayors wanted to make it compulsory for men to bathe in "skirted" bathing suits!

### Costume cover up

In the early 1900s females had to wear dark bathing suits made from flannel or flannelette, often with long, black stockings underneath. It's a wonder they didn't drown under the weight of their clothes!

BIKINIS ARE TEENY-WEENY.

### Measuring up

In the 1940s Aubrey Laidlaw was one beach inspector who many female swimmers feared. He carried a measuring tape with him, and measured swimsuits to ensure that they were regulation size!

### Two-piece ban

Alexander MacRae's manufacturing company didn't just produce his now famous Speedo swimwear for men. In the 1940s he also made two-piece swimwear for women. Of course, the beach inspectors banned the bathing suits for being indecent!

WANT MORE?

**In the early 1900s male and female bathers could not swim together.**

# STOLEN GENERATIONS

The arrival of Europeans was a catastrophe for Indigenous Australians. Their population plummeted due to disease and decimation. At the start of the 20th century, the government decided that "mixed-blood" children should be saved by being sent away to live and work with whites. In the decades to come, thousands of Indigenous children would be taken from their families without warning or explanation. These children came to be known as "the Stolen Generations."

"The blacks will have to go white."
--A.O. Neville, Chief Protector of Aborigines for Western Australia

**Child snatcher**
A.O. Neville (played by Kenneth Branagh in the film *Follow the Rabbit-Proof Fence*) was supposed to be Chief Protector of Aborigines but became their worst enemy. He wanted people to "forget that there ever were any Aborigines in Australia."

**Runaways!**
In 1931 three girls escaped from the Moore River Native Settlement and walked 1,490mi (2,400km) back to their families. Their trek became the subject of the book and film, *Follow the Rabbit-Proof Fence*.

SOMETHING TELLS ME I'M NOT THE GOOD GUY IN THIS FILM.

## SOLE SURVIVOR

Trugernanner was one of the last few survivors of another cruel episode in Australian history. When Tasmanian Aborigines fought against land-grabbing settlers in the mid-1800s, they were massacred or herded into camps. When Trugernanner died, her skeleton was displayed as a curiosity.

## Marching to remember

May 26 is National Day of Healing in Australia. On that date in 1997 a report into the Stolen Generations, titled *Bringing Them Home*, was tabled in parliament. The report revealed the full horror of what had been happening in Australia right up until the 1970s.

BLACK RIGHTS

BLACK LAND RIGHTS

## No one's land

European settlers declared Australia *terra nullius*, "no one's land." This meant they could take any land they wanted. Eddie Mabo, a Torres Strait Islander, believed his people were the traditional owners of their land. After a 10-year court battle, the concept of *terra nullius* was struck out.

## "It is time to say sorry"

Prime Minister Kevin Rudd's 2008 apology to Indigenous Australians left many in tears. Some had waited all their lives for this.

WANT MORE?

Watch Kevin Rudd's 2008 "Sorry" speech ☆ http://bit.ly/dgYsA8

# FAR OUTBACK

In the vast outback, going to the store to buy a newspaper is not a quick trip, but in the past, getting sick could get you a quick trip to heaven. Just two doctors looked after an area of about 770,000 sq miles (2 million sq km). A mercy dash from a doctor could take more than a week! Luckily, Reverend John Flynn came to the rescue. He campaigned for air ambulances in the outback and finally, in 1928, the Royal Flying Doctor Service took to the skies.

**Reverend John Flynn**

3 days to post office

18 hours to neighbor

3 weeks to Grandma's

2 hours to letter box

WOOP WOOP CREEK

10 days to beach

### Calling for help
The Royal Flying Doctor Service got off the ground in May 1928. But how could people in the outback call for help? Luckily, in 1929 Alfred Traeger invented a pedal-operated generator to power a radio receiver. Finally, fingers could do the dialing and feet could do the pedaling!

*GALAHS LOVE TO GALAH!*

### Grave concern
Flynn was spurred on by stories such as James Darcy's. In 1917 stockman Darcy fell off his horse. A postmaster operated on him with a razor and a penknife, receiving instructions by Morse code from a doctor. The doctor took 13 days to get there, but Darcy died the day before.

### Noisy neighbors
Transistorized radios allowed outback people to keep in touch. For half an hour three times a day, nurses operated the radio and passed on messages. These were known as "galah" sessions. A galah is a cockatoo that loves to chatter!

*SHOULD WE CALL IT A CHATTERBOX?*

*WHERE IS MY TEACHER?*

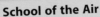

### School of the Air
The two-way radios that saved lives also helped children in the outback learn. In 1948 school lessons were broadcast from the Royal Flying Doctor Service base at Alice Springs. Back then, children had to pedal to talk to their teacher! Today, lessons come in via satellites.

Pedal radios transmitted messages by Morse code.

The Royal Flying Doctor Service runs 24 hours a day, 365 days a year.

WANT MORE?

# ANIMaL INVASION!

Every year, millions of visitors swarm to Australia, but some of the foreigners are not welcome. Although first given a passport to cross into Australia's borders, some animals have turned from animal tourist into animal terrorist. A war now rages in the wilderness with animal invaders winning the battle. Killer creatures, such as cane toads and rabbits, are out-feeding and out-breeding many of the native species. What are the invaders' weapons of mass destruction? Annihilating appetites and millions of munching mouths!

Toad Day Out is a pest-control event. But you have to hand in the cane toads alive!

**Tough old toads**
Cane toads have been known to hop away from a bushfire and pick themselves up after being run over, but they are toad toast if you put them in a fridge and then a freezer (it is the kindest way to kill them).

**TOXIC TeeTH?**
Cane toads are one amphibian you would not want to kiss. They can release toxic poison from glands on their shoulders. However, this has not put off some dentists. The poison from cane toads has been used to cure toothache.

**The bane of the cane**
In 1935 cane toads were brought to Australia to eat the cane beetles that were destroying the sugar-cane crops. But there was one big problem. The cane beetles lived at the tops of the cane stalks, and the cane toads could not jump that high. Wouldn't that make you hopping mad?

THERE ARE NO FLIES ON ME.

# WAR OF THE WAVE

In Australia, flies can make people fly into a rage. There are about 30,000 different kinds, but one kind is always flying into the face of danger. Bush flies like to feed on the secretions around people's eyes and mouths. It is such a problem that there is even a special name for when people flick a fly from their face—the "Australian salute!"

THERE ARE NO FLEAS ON ME.

RUN, THE FARMER'S COMING!

**A big bunny battle**
Rabbits arrived in Australia on the convict ships in 1788. Then in 1859, Thomas Austin was a bit of a bunny. He released about 24 rabbits into the wild. Today, hundreds of millions of rabbits massacre the vegetation and have been described as "chainsaws of the outback."

WANT MORE?

**More cane toad truths** ☆ australianmuseum.net.au/Cane-Toad

# DiGGiNG DOWN UNDER

To miners, Australia is a treasure chest of precious minerals. For centuries, miners have dug, burrowed, and blasted their way into the ground trying to get at them. Massive machines have mostly replaced muscle power in today's vast new mines but the dusty prospectors of old are not dead. They live on in Australia's opal-mining towns. These towns are Australia's answer to the Wild West. They even have old-fashioned villains—the dastardly thieves they call "ratters!"

### Opal fever

Opals were once thought to bring bad luck. In the town of Coober Pedy, they bring fever—opal fever. Anyone can stake a claim and start digging. But watch out for ratters, who sneak down the mines at night and steal other miners' opals. There are tall tales of ratters meeting a sticky end at the bottom of a disused mineshaft!

The world's biggest opal was found at Coober Pedy. It weighed 7.6lb (3.45kg)!

WITH LUCK, IT WON'T BE AN OPAL-LESS CASE.

RATS! THOSE RATTERS WILL BE AFTER THIS.

## HOSTELS ROCK!

Bed, breakfast, and bedrock—that's what you get when you stay at Coober Pedy. That's pretty cool. Particularly when you consider that the surrounding landscape is so hot and bleak that it's a favorite film location for movies about the end of the world.

**No greens**
Players at the Coober Pedy Golf Club have to cart around a piece of turf so they can tee off. At least they don't have to worry about "Keep Off the Grass" signs!

IT'S NOT MUCH, BUT IT'S "MINE!"

**Bound for the underground**
Some opal miners don't just work underground, they live there, too. Many locals in Coober Pedy have built their homes in caves and old mines to escape the boiling heat outside. You can even shop, visit a cafe, or go to church underground. That sure is life "down under!"

WANT MORE?

# SHE'LL BE RIGHT, MATE!

A friend is called a cobber, a chum, or a buddy, but the friend who sticks by you through thick and thin is a "mate." During World War I, the soldiers, or "diggers," in the Australian Army relied on their mates to survive. One such courageous digger at Gallipoli, in Turkey, was Private John Simpson. With his faithful donkey at his side, Simpson would whistle and sing as he trudged up and down Shrapnel Valley under enemy fire to carry back wounded or dying mates.

WHERE ARE YOUR MATES WHEN YOU NEED THEM?

**Simpson's mates**
Private Simpson was known as "the bloke with the donk" but there may have been more than one donkey. However, Duffy was his favorite.

In 24 days, Simpson rescued more than 300 soldiers.

**A brave mate**
Leonard Keysor had a short fuse when it came to cricket ball bombs. When the Turkish soldiers threw the ball-shaped bombs at the Australians, Keysor sometimes caught them and tossed them right back. During one battle, Keysor kept up his bomb-disposing for 50 hours!

## Cricket and mates

When the Australians were evacuated from Gallipoli over a number of nights in December 1915, sport became a real distraction. The soldiers waiting for their turn to be evacuated played cricket during the day to make everything seem like normal.

## Medical mates

Australian nurses often had to deal with bullets and bombs as well as bandages. In France in 1917, four Australian nurses received bravery awards for rescuing patients from a burning building.

The beach they played cricket on was called Shell Green!

CRICKET'S A BOMB!

## MORE ON MATES

On December 24, 1914, after some German soldiers started singing Christmas carols, the two sides had a truce and became mates. They talked, drank, and swapped simple gifts. But on Christmas Day, they were back to war!

EAT ME, DON'T EAT MY MATE!

## Man's best mate

During World War I, Rolf the dog was best friends with some Australian troops, thanks to the smell of some bacon they were cooking. Before that, Rolf had been best mates with the German enemy!

WANT MORE?

**Australian War Memorial official site** ☆ www.awm.gov.au

# THE LIGHTNING HORSE

Phar Lap was Australia's wonder horse. His name meant "lightning" and he ran like lightning, too. Harry Telford, a down-on-his-luck Australian trainer, bought the horse in New Zealand in 1928 without ever laying eyes on him. But Telford's luck was about to change. What lay hidden inside the big red horse would eventually make Phar Lap win many races, as well as win over the hearts of the Australian people.

NO ONE'S GOING TO STEAL MY THUNDER.

Won 37 out of 51 races

### The legend lives on

The Jonas Brothers, famous New York taxidermists, preserved Phar Lap. They even glued pieces of rope into the exact places where his veins had been. Their work was not in vain. People gasped at how lifelike he looked.

## A CHAMP REVAMP

In 2010, when Phar Lap's skeleton and his hide stood side by side for an exhibition, it was clear the skeleton needed an extreme makeover. Assembled in 1938 by a taxidermist who was no expert in horse anatomy, the skeleton had knock knees, a drooping spine, and a sagging head! But in March 2012 Phar Lap's skeleton finally stood tall—7in (18cm) taller.

> I LOOK AS IF I HAVE BEEN STRUCK BY LIGHTNING!

### Loved by all

After his death in 1932, Phar Lap's remains went to three different places: his hide to Melbourne, his heart to Canberra and his skeleton to New Zealand. But in 2000 Phar Lap didn't move like lightning when he was relocated 0.6 mi (1 km). It took more than five hours!

The saying "you have a heart as big as Phar Lap" means you are very brave.

> I WAS HARD TO BEAT.

### A big-hearted horse

Phar Lap definitely had the X-factor. His heart weighed 14lb (6.35kg), whereas an average horse's heart weighs about 8.8lb (4kg). Phar Lap's bloodline can be traced back to an English horse named Eclipse. When Eclipse died in 1789, amazingly, his heart also weighed 14lb (6.35kg).

### Shot to fame

In November 1930 a man shot at, but missed, Phar Lap as he returned from training. There were two suspicious men in a car before the shooting. One hid his face with a newspaper; the other with a handkerchief.

WANT MORE?

**Phar Lap's heart** ☆ www.nma.gov.au/collections/highlights/phar-laps-heart

# LiFE iN A POCKET

Life can be pretty pleasant in a pouch. It is warm, safe, and secure. Some animals in Australia start out life in a pouch after taking a short but treacherous journey there as soon as they are born. These pouch mammals are called marsupials. Some babies have plenty of leg room as they have the whole pouch to themselves. For others that share it with brothers and sisters, there is less elbow room! But no matter how snug as a bug in a rug pouch babies might be, as they get older, they pop out of the pouch and one day never pop back.

THERE'S ELBOW ROOM.
JUST NO LEG ROOM!

COME ON,
IT'S TIME
TO HOP OUT!

### Pocket time
Rock wallabies have striped tails and fuzzy feet, and belong to the same family as kangaroos. For most marsupials, the time when they first leave the pouch to when they never go back inside is usually a couple of months. But the joeys of rock wallabies are like little pocket rockets. They stop hopping back in after about a week.

THESE OVERALLS
DON'T HAVE
ANY MARSUPIUMS!

## Pocket fight

Tasmanian devils live on the Australian island of Tasmania. These fierce animals are not angelic! They will fight tooth and nail over food and mates, and when threatened. A female gives birth to about 20 to 30 young at a time, but has only four teats in her pouch. Only the fiercest little devils survive.

I WANT TO LIVE IN A POCKET.

The pouch is called a marsupium.

## BULLDOZERS OF THE BUSH

When your full-time job is digging, having a pouch that faces forward might be an occupational hazard, so a female wombat's pouch faces to the back. This helps prevent dirt and water from entering the pouch. However, there might be other hazards for the baby wombat back there!

### Room with a view

Life facing backward in a pouch may not have the most pleasant outlook, but you would certainly be kept busy. Wombats can deposit up to 100 cube-shaped droppings a night. They use them as "signposts" to mark their territory. They are the perfect poop because they do not roll away!

WANT MORE?

Koalas have rear-facing pouches, which seems dangerous for a tree-climber!

# GOLD AND GALS

In 1851, when gold was discovered in Australia, many folks hot-footed it to seek their fortune. And hot feet is what they got as they traipsed the dusty deserts to the diggings. They were not likely to get lost, though. Along the way, there was a great trail of tablecloths, axes, blankets, and teakettles that people had thrown aside to lighten their load. Adventurous women also followed the trail, and before long, "girl power" struck the goldfields!

> IS HE ARTHUR OR MARTHA?

### Licenses and ladies
Diggers had to buy a gold license and have it on them at all times. Even men on the goldfields who didn't mine had to have one. However, women were exempt. No wonder some men dressed as women when the police came. They were never "frilled" to see them!

> NO "COFFEE" FOR ME. I'M A TEA-TOTALLER.

### Trouble brewing
It was illegal to sell alcohol at the diggings, but some women started up "coffee tents," where they sold "cool drinks" to the thirsty diggers. But isn't coffee hot? It soon was. The police often set the traders' tents on fire. How mean-spirited of them!

> MY COFFEE TENT IS THIS WAY.

## Darling of the diggers

Lola Montes headed from California to Australia in 1855. She was famous for her spider dance. She was so popular that the diggers threw lumps of gold onto the stage. What little gems!

# THE GOLDEN GIRLS

Before the first Australian gold rush, gold buried in quartz was displayed in Sydney stores, and considered "queer stuff." However, no one thought it was funny when gold fetched big money. Some notable nuggets sported female names:

☆ Blanche Barkly: **109lb (49kg)** (1857)

☆ Viscountess Canterbury: **57lb (26kg)** (1870)

☆ Leila: **42lb (19kg)** (1907)

> THE GOLDEN RULE IS DON'T GET YOUR SHOES MUDDY.

> Australian gold miners were called "diggers." A digger's wife was sometimes called a "diggeress."

### The golden lottery

"Confound it! I've broken my pick!" cried John Deason on February 5, 1869. He had just hit the largest nugget in the world. The "Welcome Stranger" weighed 210 lb (95 kg). That night, he kept it on his table under a cloth and threw a party. History doesn't say if women were invited.

## THE PETTICOAT FLAG

When diggers yell "Eureka," it means they've struck gold. But in 1854 at Eureka, it meant a revolution. The diggers hoisted the Eureka flag and rebelled against the gold license system. Some people believe three women carefully sewed the flag from fine blue wool, often used to make petticoats. A trooper who seized the flag after the battle was not so careful. He stamped on it and thrust his bayonet into it!

WANT MORE?

**Australian gold rushes** ☆ www.sbs.com.au/gold

# HULLABALOO AT THE HARBOR

Meet the radical and rule-breaking Sydney Opera House. You might not know it today, but when it was first designed, some people said that it couldn't and shouldn't be built—and it almost wasn't. But the Sydney Opera House really has plenty to sing about and plenty to smile about, too. It is one of the most photographed buildings on the planet. Outside, it is a meeting and greeting place. Inside, the music venues host operas, ballets, and dramas. There has even been a flea circus!

## The master of the piece

When Australia ran an international contest to find a design for an opera house, 233 entries from 32 countries flooded in. Jørn Utzon, an architect from Denmark, took out the top prize in 1957. A smart sailor, Utzon created a radical design that looked like a ship with billowing sails. But the project wasn't always smooth sailing. It took Utzon a couple of years alone to work out how to build the roof "sails."

Jørn Utzon

At first, the winning design sat in the rejection pile.

THAT DOG COLLAR IS NOTHING TO SING ABOUT.

## BARKING MAD

Concerts are part of daily life at the Sydney Opera House, but what about a canine concert? In 2010 the world's first concert for dogs was 20 minutes of hound-howling and toe-tapping fun for about 1,000 dogs and their owners. To the humans, it sounded like ear-piercing, high-pitched whistles. To the hounds, it was heavenly harmony.

WHEN DOES THE FLEA CIRCUS START?

> I LOOK LIKE AN ORANGE.

### Opera orange

Like Isaac Newton with his falling apple, architect Jørn Utzon had a real "Eureka" moment when he peeled an orange and saw the three-dimensional segments. There are 10 roof vaults on the Sydney Opera House, forming an "orange," or a perfect sphere, if they were all put together.

### The tile file

At a quick count, there are more than one million tiles on the Opera House's roof. Luckily, they are self-cleaning when it rains. The tiles look white from afar, but a closer look reveals they consist of cream matt tiles and white glazed tiles. Fancy a look-alike roof on your house? There's nothing stopping you. They are still available. Just ask for the "Sydney tile."

> I HOPE IT RAINS. THERE ARE MILES OF TILES!

### VIVID IMAGINATION

In May and June, Vivid Sydney, a festival of light and music, sure paints the town red—and every other color of the rainbow. At night, colorful creations are projected onto the sails of the Opera House. But when it is not being lit up with special effects, there's no need to feel blue. The white and cream tiles change color in the natural sunlight.

WANT MORE?

# THE FLYING FRUIT FLIES

Children as young as eight have been flying on the trapeze and flying through the air since 1979 when the Flying Fruit Fly Circus first opened its (tent) doors. But they haven't swapped their classroom for the big top. They go to school there, too. It's Australia's only full-time children's circus school.

**Fruit fly warning**
Not all fruit flies are welcome at the circus. Some species of fruit flies are a pest in Australia. The circus took its name from the fruit fly checkpoints on the border between Victoria and New South Wales.

There are more than 80 kinds of fruit flies in Australia.

Fruit Fly Free Zone 50 km Ahead

**A cool school**
Even homework is fun at the circus school. Tumbling, tightrope walking, and trapeze are just some of the great after-school subjects!

### Growing up in the circus

When Fruit Fly performers grow up, they can simply flee to another circus. Circus Oz started up in 1977. Its founding performers were so keen to start that they sewed their own circus tent!

I'M FLYING LIKE A FRUIT FLY.

### Famous fruit fly

Some former Fruit Flies have become famous outside of the circus ring. Emma George, once a trapeze artist, learned to fly over the pole-vault bar, and set 12 world records!

WANT MORE?

Flying Fruit Fly Circus official site ☆ www.fruitflycircus.com.au

CRIKEY, HOLD YOUR HORSES.

Steve wrestled his first croc when he was nine years old.

# WHAT A LITTLE BEAUTY

Crikey! Steve Irwin was a croc-catching, snake-snatching wildlife expert who loved the deadliest and most dangerous animals in the world. His nickname was "the Crocodile Hunter," but he didn't kill crocs, he wrestled and captured them to save them from the shoot-to-kill crocodile hunters. Steve Irwin's parents had a passion for protecting Australia's deadly predators, and he grew up to be an adventurous wildlife warrior. In 2006 Steve Irwin died as he lived—in nature's danger zone.

## Look, don't touch

Steve was given a 13 ft- (4 m-) long scrub python for his sixth birthday, which he fondly named Fred. It's a shame that Steve never got to play with his pet, but the snake could easily have eaten him. Now that's what you call a s-s-s-snack attack!

A scrub python

## WORDS OF A WARRIOR

**aggro**—aggressive
**beaut**—great or fantastic
**bloke**—a man
**crikey**—an expression of astonishment
**yakka**—work (catching crocs
    is hard yakka!)

### Killers in the cooler

During a game of schoolboy cricket, Steve became bored and wandered off to check out the wildlife. He ended up catching seven deadly snakes and putting them in the bus driver's cooler bin for the ride home. No wonder snakes are cold-blooded!

BUS TRIPS ARE BORING. WANT TO PLAY SNAKES AND LADDERS?

ARE WE THERE YET?

CRIKEY

Australia Zoo
Home of The Crocodile Hunter

*A roadside sign for Australia Zoo*

### Crocs rock!

By 1973, because their bedrooms were bursting at the seams with animals, Steve's parents opened up a wildlife park. In 1991 Steve took it over and it became the Australia Zoo. The attraction that gets everyone crying "Crikey!" is the Crocoseum, where the crowd watches crocs plunge and lunge for some lunch.

### Road-kill rescue

As a boy, Steve probably never got bored on car rides. His mother used to stop whenever she saw any road kill to make sure that there was not a baby joey inside the dead kangaroo's pouch. Steve was often late for school because of their roadside rescues. Extra credit for that excuse!

### Emu antics

One of Steve's boyhood pets was an emu named Egg Head, but Egg Head was a bit of a featherbrain. He used to gobble up marbles during games. Steve had to wait a week before they came out the other end. But once they were washed down, they were as good as new.

CARS MAKE ME HOPPING MAD!

WANT MORE?

Australia Zoo official site ☆ www.australiazoo.com.au

# THE CaMEL TRaiN

In 1846, Harry the Camel was one of the first camels to set foot in Australia. Later, thousands of camels arrived and became Australia's "ships of the desert." Soon camel trains—along with their cameleers, who came from places such as Afghanistan—hauled goods and people. Then a real train replaced the camel trains that trekked from Adelaide to Alice Springs. The train pulled out of Adelaide Railway Station in 1929. Aboard were about 100 passengers who were thrilled they didn't have to go by camel!

> WE DIDN'T GIVE WAY. WE STOPPED.

### The road code
There was often great rivalry between the cameleers and the bullock teamsters who also hauled goods for a living. One cameleer was shot and wounded because a bullock teamster believed he failed to give way!

## TiME OF THE LiNE
Today, the Ghan railroad runs from Adelaide to Darwin. The railroad was completed in several stages.

| 1878 First tracks laid in Adelaide in South Australia | 1891 Reaches Oodnadatta in South Australia | 1929 Reaches Alice Springs in Central Australia | 2004 Reaches Darwin in Northern Australia |

## A lengthy line

The first train lines in the big cities, such as Sydney and Melbourne, went the grand distance of a few kilometers. So it must have come as a shock to the railroad builders in 1878 when they had to build tracks thousands of kilometers across the continent. In 2004, 126 years after the first sleepers were laid, the Ghan railroad reached Darwin. The end of the line was 1,851mi (2,979km) from the start.

The train was first called the Afghan Express. Later it was the Ghan Express. Then it was just the Ghan.

I'M A MITE-Y, BITE-Y TERMITE.

## Trouble on the track

On the Old Ghan line, wooden sleepers stretched as far as the eye could see. However, there was one slight problem. Well, thousands of slight problems—termites. Termites feasted on the wooden sleepers. Luckily, in 1980 along came new concrete sleepers. Eat your heart out, termites!

Darwin

———— Current route
- - - - - - Old route

DON'T SHOOT. I'M BILLY THE KID!

Alice Springs

Oodnadatta

## Train in the rain

Flash floods often washed away parts of the Old Ghan railroad. One time, the train got stuck for two weeks and couldn't budge. The story goes that the train driver shot wild goats for his hungry passengers. Floods could turn a two-day journey from Adelaide to Alice Springs into a two-week trip. So people dubbed the Old Ghan "the train you can walk faster than." Wouldn't that get on your goat!

Adelaide

WANT MORE?

Camels in Australian exploration ☆ www.burkeandwills.net.au/Camels/index.htm

# OFF THE MAP

In 1860, the race was on to be the first to walk off the map, and cross Australia from south to north to unlock the secrets of the great Australian desert. Flush with gold-rush money, the state of Victoria put up the cash for a daring expedition by camel, unimaginatively called the Victorian Exploring Expedition. To lead the expedition they chose an eccentric Irishman named Burke. It was a choice they would regret!

The expedition's supplies included 70 gallons (270L) of rum--for the camels!

I AM TIRED OF HUMPING THIS GEAR AROUND.

## THE MAIN MEN

There were many expedition members. Some didn't last long because Burke had a habit of firing people whenever they got on his nerves.

I WILL CROSS AUSTRALIA OR PERISH IN THE ATTEMPT!

**Robert O'Hara Burke**

**Leader**
Burke had no experience of exploring and was once described as being unable to tell "the north from the south in broad daylight."

HOW DO YOU HANDLE A CAMEL?

**John Wills**

**Second in command**
Wills was a surveyor (thankfully with a good sense of direction). His fatal mistake was trusting in Burke's oddball leadership skills.

VERY CAREFULLY!

**John King**

**Camel handler**
King was appointed a camel handler despite knowing nothing about camels.

**Outbound route**

**Return route**

FLINDERS RIVER

CORELLA CREEK

KING CREEK

COOPER CREEK

SWAN HILL

MELBOURNE

### 4. Dig!
Burke, Wills, and King find a tree marked with the word "Dig." Buried beneath it is a stash of food. But it is not enough to get the men back home. Burke and Wills soon die, and the last survivor, King, never fully recovers from his ordeal.

### 3. Success?
The four men almost reach the far north. Only dense mangroves prevent them from getting to the coast. Starving and exhausted, just three survivors stagger back to the Cooper Creek camp. They discover the rest of the expedition has given up and left for home that morning!

### 2. Snake snack
From Cooper Creek, Burke, Wills, King, and one other strike out for the northern coast—a round trip of 930mi (1,500km)! Food runs out, and Burke gets the runs after eating a snake!

### 1. Camel chaos
The expedition's send-off in Melbourne is chaotic. One crazed camel careers through the crowd, knocking a woman off her horse and breaking her leg.

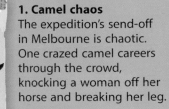

**WANT MORE?**

**The gateway to Burke and Wills** ☆ burkeandwills.slv.vic.gov.au

# INDEX

NOT-FOR-PARENTS
# AUSTRALIA
## EVERYTHING YOU EVER WANTED TO KNOW

**1st Edition**
**Published September 2012**

Conceived by Weldon Owen in partnership with Lonely Planet
Produced by Weldon Owen Publishing
Northburgh House, 10 Northburgh Street
London, EC1V 0AT, UK

weldonowenpublishing.com

Copyright © 2012 Weldon Owen Publishing

WELDON OWEN
PUBLISHING

**WELDON OWEN LTD**

**Managing Director** Sarah Odedina

**Publisher** Corinne Roberts

**Creative Director** Sue Burk

**Sales Director** Laurence Richard

**Sales Manager, North America** Ellen Towell

**Project Editor** Shan Wolody

**Assistant Researcher** Peter Rees

**Designer** Katy Wall

**Design Assistant** Haylee Bruce

**Index** Puddingburn Publishing Services

**Production Director** Dominic Saraceno

**Production Controller** Tristan Hanks

**Published by**

Lonely Planet Publications Pty Ltd ABN 36 005 607 983
90 Maribyrnong St, Footscray, Victoria 3011, Australia

ISBN 978-1-7432-1422-0

Printed in China

**A WELDON OWEN PRODUCTION**

**Credits and acknowledgments**

Key tl=top left; tcl=top center left; tc=top center; tcr=top center right; tr=top right;
cl=center left; c=center; cr=center right; bl=bottom left; bcl=bottom center left;
bc=bottom center; bcr=bottom center right; br=bottom right; bg = background.

4cr, 8bc, 10tr, 11bcl, 18bc, 19tc, 24cl, 47br, 48cr, 50cl, 68cr, 72-73tc, 74bl, 78-79tc, 80bl,
81tc, 88tc, 89cl **Alamy**; 45tr **AP Photo/Mark Pardew**; 60tl **Auscape International**;
9bl, 16-17tc, 28-29c, 30-31c, 38cr, 38-39tc, 48bc, 49cl, 59bcl, 71c, 73cl **Corbis**; 11cl,
12bl, 25bc, br, 27c, 39bcr, br, 40cl, 41bc, bcl, tcl, 57bl, 59tl, 71tc, 77br, 80br, tr, 90c
94bcl, 95bcr **Dreamstime**; 83cl **The Eureka Centre, Ballarat**; 9tc, 16bl, 17bc, 22bc,
31bc, c, 34r, 45tcl, 47c, cl, tr, 50cr, tr, 51c, tc, 54bl, 54-55tc, 59br, 69tl, 75bl, 79cr, 81bl,
84bl, 86bl, cr, 87cl, cr, tc **Getty Images**; 2cr, 2-3bc, 3bcl, bcr, tc, 8-9c, 9br, c, 11bcr, bg,
12b, cl, cr, 13c, r, 14bl, 14-15bg, 16c, cl, 18c, 19bc, 21bc, 23bc, c, 24cr, 25c, 26bl, 27cr, tc,
tc, 28bl, br, c, 28-29tc, 29bc, cl, tc, tcr, tr, 30bc, 31tr, 32bc, 33bc, 34bl, 35bc, bg, br, cr,
36bl, cl, 37bc, 38bc, c, tr, 38-39bg, 39c, cl, tc, 40-41c, 41cr, 42bc, bc, c, 43bc, bcr, br, cr, r,
tcr, 44c, 44-45b, tc, 45br, c, cr, 47br, tc, 48-49t, 50br, c, 51bc, 52c, 53tl, 55cr, 57bcr, 58tr,
58-59c, 59tcl, tr, 60bc, 62tl, 63br, cl, tc, tr, 64c, 67c, 71cr, 72cl, 73tr, 74bc, br, 77cr, r, tl,
78cl, 79bl, 81bcr, tcr, 83br, cr, 85bcr, cr, 86-87bg, 89bc, bl, br, cr, 90b, 90-91tc, 91br, c, cr,
92tc, tl, 94bl, br, br, 95bc, bc, br, tc, tcl and all repeated image motifs **iStockphoto.
com**; 2bl, 10c, 12-13tr, 13cl, 20tr, 20-21c, tc, 21cl, cr, 24bc, 24-25tr, 35cl, 39cr, tr, 45bcl,
49bl, tc, 52bc, cl, 54cr, 57cl, 60-61tc, 61bc, br, cl, tr, 64br, 64-65tr, 65bc, 66bl, 69bc,
74-75tc, 75cr, 82br, cl, 84-85c, 90bc, 90-91tc, 91tc **Lonely Planet**; 69tc **Museum
Victoria**; 46-47tl **NHPA/Photoshot**; 3cr, 9bc, 10bc, 11cr, tc, 12c, tc, 13cr, 15tr, 18cl,
19tcr, 20c, 23br, c, cr, tr, 26br, c, 27bc, bc, bg, 28cl, 30br, 37bcr, cl, tcr, 38br, 41tc, 42cl,
48cl, 48-49bg, 49c, tcr, 55c, 58cr, 59cr, tc, 60c, 63c, 64tc, 67cr, 70tr, 72bc, 73cr, 77tc,
79bc, cl, 85bcl, tc, 88br, 94bc, bc, tcr, 95bl, bl, tcr, tl **Shutterstock**.

**Australian War Memorial** 76tr J06392; **National Archives of Australia** 9cr A6180,
23/8/74/3; 69tr A9626, 162; 70c A6135, K12/1/77/28; **National Library of Australia**
12c F. Werner, vn3700377; tc Anon, an23259464; 14tc Geoffrey Ingleton, an6153054;
14-15c John Allcot, an7891482; 15bc E.W. Searle, an23796165; 42cl Henry
Macbeth-Raeburn, an9846228; 42-43tc V. Woodthorpe, an7896980; 49bcr Anon,
an21971935; 56bl Fred Hardie, vn4557471; 57bc Vandyck Studio, ms9065-5; tcr Anon,
an22199070; 68bl Charles Alfred Woolley, an23795214; 70tr John Flynn, an24680767;
82tr Paul Henrion, an7095172; 92c J.C. Armytage & Nicholas Chevalier, an7372844;
**Mitchell Library, State Library of NSW** 62br PXE 787/no.20; 63tl Home and Away
– 12036; 84c Australian Photographic Agency. [d7_03870]; **State Library of
Queensland** 71cl neg no. 166304; 92bl image no. 7871-0001-0036; **Pictures
Collection, State Library of Victoria** 18-19c A/S03/07/80/14; 26cr H42641/4; tr
H91.94; 29bcr H99.201/514; 31br H2000.200/1833; 36cr H13188/verso; tc
IAN18/06/70/116; 37cr H19984; tcr H96.160/70; 52cr IAN24/09/64/1; 64bl
H99.201/2518, c IAM25/08/62/145; 67tr H2010.18/62; 78bc H91.160/287; 82-83c
H81.23/9; 90cl H2002.199/963; 92bc H5412, tr H90.90/12; **State Library of Western
Australia** 68c 226017PD.

Cover illustrations by **Chris Corr**.

17bcr, tcr, 94tr **Thomas Bayley/The Art Agency**; 1br, 4-5cl, 6-7c, 7bc, 93tl, c, cr, bc,
bg, 94tc **Chris Corr**; 66-67c **Rob Davis/The Art Agency**; 58bl **Alan Ewart**; 76-77c
**Geri Ford/The Art Agency**; 16cr **Mick Posen/The Art Agency**; 32-33c, 33cr, 53c
**Dave Smith/The Art Agency**.

All illustrations and maps copyright 2012 Weldon Owen Publishing

## LONELY PLANET OFFICES

**Australia Head Office**
Locked Bag 1, Footscray, Victoria 3011
Phone 03 8379 8000  Fax 03 8379 8111

**USA**
150 Linden St, Oakland, CA 94607
Phone 510 250 6400  Toll free 800 275 8555  Fax 510 893 8572

**UK**
Media Centre, 201 Wood Lane, London W12 7TQ
Phone 020 8433 1333  Fax 020 8702 0112

lonelyplanet.com/contact